Pandora's

A Greek Myth

Contents

Chapter One

The Mysterious Box   2

Chapter Two

Trouble Brewing   10

Chapter Three

Help!   20

Chapter Four

Myths Today   26

Chapter One

The Mysterious Box

Once upon a time, there was
an orphan child named
Epimetheus (Epa-mee-thee-us).
Because he had no one to tell him
what to do, Epimetheus played.
He didn't read books.
He didn't write letters.
He just played and played.

One day, another orphan
was sent to keep
Epimetheus company.
Her name was Pandora.
She was a curious girl.

The first thing Pandora saw
when she got to Epimetheus'
hut was a beautiful box.
The box was made of bronze.
It was big and shiny and golden.

Pandora said, "Epimetheus,
what's in the box?"

Epimetheus answered,
"I don't know. That is
a secret. Someone left it here,
but I don't know what's inside it."

Pandora frowned.
She was very curious
about what was in the box.

"Where did it come from? Who gave it to you?" Pandora asked eagerly.

Epimetheus shook his head and replied, "That is a secret."

Pandora begged. Pandora pleaded.
Pandora stamped her feet.

However, Epimetheus would not tell her anything else about the box.

"How can I tell you, Pandora?" said Epimetheus. "I don't know any more about what is inside than you do."

Pandora said, "Well, we could open it and see for ourselves!"

"We are not *allowed* to open the box, Pandora," Epimetheus said.

Chapter Two

Trouble Brewing

Days and days went by.

Pandora and Epimetheus

became good friends.

They played in the forest.

They ran races.

They made tiny seed cakes

for the birds and other animals.

They made mud pies.

However, Pandora could not stop
thinking about the box.

"How did the box get here?"
she asked Epimetheus.

Epimetheus told her all about a
messenger with wings on his feet
who had brought the box.

"Oh, that must have been Hermes!" said Pandora. "He was the one who brought me here. Maybe Hermes brought the box for us! Maybe the box is full of new clothes and toys. Maybe it has presents inside. Let's have a little peek," she said.

Epimetheus did not want to open the box. He went outside to play and left Pandora alone.

Pandora looked at the box.

She walked around the box.

She looked at the latch.
She knelt down in front
of the box and fiddled
with the latch. It clicked open.

"I will open up the lid
just a tiny bit," she said.
And she did.

As soon as Pandora opened the box, a terrible thing happened.

All of the great and scary troubles of the world started to fly out of the box. Sickness, misery, and cruelty escaped and flew around the hut.

"Help!" Pandora cried.

She tried to push the lid
of the box back down,
but she could not keep
the great and scary troubles
from escaping.

Finally, she jumped up
and, using all of her strength,
shut the lid.

Chapter Three

Help!

Epimetheus heard Pandora
calling for help.
He ran to the hut to see
what was wrong.

All the great and scary troubles
of the world circled around
the hut like a mighty black cloud.

"Oh no! Maybe Pandora
opened the box!" he yelled.

He ran inside the hut.

Pandora was sitting
on top of the box.

"What happened, Pandora?"
Epimetheus asked.

"It was horrible!" she replied.
"I lifted the lid just a tiny bit
and all the great and scary
troubles escaped."

Pandora and Epimetheus watched
as all the great and scary troubles
of the world swarmed away
like giant bees.

"Well, there goes trouble!"
said Epimetheus with a sigh.

Pandora felt something bump
inside the box.

She jumped down and lifted
the lid of the box one more time.

Inside the box, there was
only one thing left – hope.

Hope remained when all
the great and scary troubles
of the world escaped.

Chapter Four

Myths Today

A myth is a story that has been told for a long time.

In ancient Greece, the story about Pandora was just one tiny part of many myths about life.

Because these stories were told out loud, instead of being written down, there are many different versions of "Pandora's Box". Sometimes the box is a jar. Sometimes it is Epimetheus, not Pandora, who opens up the box.

In some stories, Pandora and Epimetheus are married and, in other stories, they are children.

In the Greek myths, all of the characters had names that had special meanings.

The god that made Pandora gave her all the gifts of beauty, cunning, and charm. The name *Pandora* means "all gifts".

The name *Epimetheus* means "hindsight". Hindsight is what you have after you have learned a lesson. Then you understand what you didn't know before.

Today, when a person says something is a "Pandora's box", this means that, even though something looks nice,
it's a whole lot of trouble once you take a closer look.

Some people also say, "There's always hope."
Now you can think about the myth of Pandora's Box whenever you hear those expressions!

From the Author

My mother told me the Greek myths. I am a curious person, so the story of "Pandora's Box" seemed very scary to me when I was younger. Now my children are curious about the story and can read it.

Diana Short Yurkovic

From the Illustrator

Of all the Greek myths I read as a boy, "Pandora's Box" stands out the most. It was fun to imagine what it might have looked like when Pandora was puzzled by the box – and afterwards, too! What do you think it might have looked like?

Steve Clark